THE AUTOBIOGRAPHY OF A
NATIVE HAWAIIAN PEARL HARBOR SURVIVOR

COUNTING MY BLESSINGS

—— HERB WEATHERWAX ——

By: Herb Weatherwax
As told to Cliff Reid

PACIFIC
HISTORIC PARKS
★ Remember ★ Honor ★ Understand ★

www.pacifichistoricparks.org

ISBN: 978-1-936626-55-7

Printed in Hong Kong

Published by Pacific Historic Parks
1 Arizona Memorial Place
Honolulu, Hawaii 96818
www.pacifichistoricparks.org

DEDICATION

I dedicate this book first to my family and then to all others I have known throughout my lifetime. There have been so many, and I can honestly say that I have learned from every one of you, even from the small children. Thank you all for sharing the times of my life with me—past, present and future.

TABLE OF CONTENTS

Introduction..1

In the Beginning...3

The School of Hard Knocks....................................7

Family Matters..11

"We Are at War!"...13

Keesler Field and Camp Shelby..........................17

Hell on Earth..19

Making My Way..27

Lehua Christina Lee Loy.....................................29

The Philippines...33

Weatherwax Electric..35

"God, help me!"...37

Kailua Home Service, Inc...................................39

Eddie..41

Going Out and Doing It......................................45

Around Home...49

To Russia with Love...51

New Experiences and Old Memories.................53

So, That's It!..55

INTRODUCTION

As I have advanced in years, I have had the urge to record my experiences, both for myself and to share with others who might be interested in my world and life. I am always learning from others and thought that someone might pick up one or two little insights from what I have gone through.

With these thoughts in mind, I tried to get my own story down on paper several years ago, but I didn't get very far with it. I am a verbal person. I enjoy talking to people and, if they are willing to listen, I am happy to relate my experiences with them. I am not a writer, but I knew that writing my story down was really the only good way to pass it along.

The thought of having someone help me with my story never occurred to me, but my daughter-in-law Carrie, wanting to do something special for me for my 80th birthday, hired a writing service for me as a gift. I appreciated it very much. Carrie made arrangements with Cliff Reid and, before I knew it, we had finished the interviews for this book. Cliff edited and reorganized the verbal material and combined it with the little written information that I had.

This process brought out memories that had been in the back of my mind. People my age tend to reminisce about their life, but eventually their experiences are just forgotten when they pass. Here is something that will carry on. The thoughts I have put in this book come from me.

Working on my story was a really enjoyable process and I am glad it came together. I feel that I have accomplished a lot over the years, but finishing this book brought my life into focus. Now, I can be happy and joyous that it's done.

IN THE BEGINNING

I'll start my story by first talking about my roots.

My father Clarence Herbert Weatherwax had wanderlust. He was the first of six children and left his hometown of Waterloo, Iowa as a young man. First, he went to the state of Washington and eventually traveled to Hawaii. He was looking for adventure and for work.

He met my mother Anna Malamanui Keliihoomalu in Hawaii and they were married in 1912. He was 29 at the time and she was between 16 and 18 years of age. Sadly, I don't know my mother's birth date or any information about her family.

My older brother Edwin Keliihoomalu was born in 1915 and I was born in 1917. I was named Herbert, after my grandfather, but was not given a middle name.

My father was killed in an industrial accident in 1917 while working for Hawaiian Dredging Company at Pearl Harbor. I was only 3 months old at the time and I do not have any memories of him. When he was killed, my mother took my older brother and me from Honolulu to the Puna District of Hawaii Island where her family lived. She had no other source of support. The company my father worked for had a life insurance policy that paid out monthly. They sent us twenty-five dollars every month, half for me and the other half for my brother.

My mother, brother and I moved in and out of different relatives' homes. We never stayed in one location. We must have moved five or six times in the first five years of my life.

My mother remarried when I was about 5 years old. We moved in with my step-father William Kanui. He had a duplex unit and, for a change, we had our own place. Our duplex was across the road from a soda-water factory and a blacksmith shop. Once we were settled in, another family moved in with us. That's how it was; we all supported one another.

One year after my mother remarried, she had another baby, my half brother William Kanui, Jr. A few years later, she had another son, Joseph Kanui. The family was then complete.

...

When I was about seven years old, I was out playing with a Japanese boy who lived with his grandmother in another duplex unit. There was little vehicle traffic in those days so we would often play in the road. That day, we were throwing a stick and chasing after it. I threw the stick across the street and my friend ran for it. That's when I saw the car coming, a Model T bread wagon. I tried to grab my friend, but I missed. The car hit and killed him right before my eyes.

Afterwards, they called me to the police station to talk to me about what happened. I heard that the driver had been drinking. The grandma of the boy would cry all the time and call out his name, Kenichi. She had been raising him and missed him terribly. Sometimes she would call me over and talk about what happened. The incident stands out in my mind. I'll never forget that name.

...

My stepfather became ill and died in 1926. After four years of marriage and two more children, my mother, still a young woman, became a widow for a second time.

After my stepfather passed away, we again moved in with relatives. In 1927, when I was 10 years old, our family qualified for a Hawaiian Homestead property. As soon as our new house was completed, my mother, brother, two half brothers, and I moved to the Keaukaha Homestead Lands on the outskirts of Hilo. Not long after we moved, my mother met Joseph Kahauolopua. He and his children moved into our tiny house and it became very cramped. Although they didn't marry, he was like a stepfather to me and supported the family. He and my mother fought quite a bit and my home life at that early stage was not very pleasant.

The house in Keaukaha was a one-room house with an open gable roof. No ceiling at all, just something to keep the rain out. The one big room had a separate area for the kitchen and there was a little porch. My brother and I shared one bed, and my mother and two half brothers slept on the floor.

There was no stove in our house. Instead, we had a couple of rocks placed outside with metal bars across them. We would build a fire underneath and place the food across the bars. We didn't have running water, either. In those days, one of the staple foods was salted salmon from Alaska, which was shipped in large barrels. We used the barrels to collect water and that was our water source. There was a spring not far away where my mother would wash clothes and then hang them on the bushes to dry. Later, a road and water line was built by our place. A pipe ran into our yard with a spigot on the end and we would use it to wash, but there was no hot water.

Our outhouse was built over underground lava tubes. All you had to do was locate one of these tubes, knock a hole in it, and put the outhouse over it! There would be spider webs in there and it wasn't too pleasant!

Hawaiian is the first language I heard because my mother, my adult relatives and my mother's common law husband were all pure Hawaiian. I could understand Hawaiian, but couldn't speak it. I spoke Pidgin English, which evolved over time out of all of the different nationalities living in the Hawaiian Islands.

Keaukaha is a lush tropical area along the coast, and our house was just two blocks away from the ocean. When I was a kid, I practically lived in the water and became quite a swimmer. The ocean was our food supply. We caught fish, crabs, and all kinds of things.

A group of us kids used to fish together. The old style goggles wouldn't fit my face properly so I wasn't able to dive too deep. As a consequence, I wasn't able to spearfish very well. My job in the group was to be a "string man." I'd have a float and the other guys would dive down, spear a fish, and then come up and throw it to me. I would string it up on a long cord attached to a float. We used a float so that if sharks came around and smelled the fish, they would go towards the float instead of us, giving us time to swim for shore. One of the older kids would supervise things and keep an eye out for sharks.

Unlike fishing, we often crabbed alone or in pairs. There were a lot of crabs back then. We would take a coconut palm leaf and attach it to bamboo with a piece of thread in between. We would brush the thread over the crab's eyes and when its eyes closed on the string, you would toss the whole rig into the air with the crab attached. The crab would open its eyes midair and we'd catch it in a bag. It sounds strange, but it worked well.

Another method we used was to tie a limpet or opihi to the end of the string and jiggle it in front of a crab hole until it would grab the bait. Then, we'd toss it up in the air and again catch it in the bag. We used to gather limpets off of the rocks with a little scraper. When I was young, they were very plentiful.

To supplement what we were able to harvest from the ocean, we would plant sweet potatoes in little hollows in the lava rock. We would collect soil that we could find in the area. You'd be surprised how rich it was!

We would also pick guava and breadfruit off the trees when they were in season. We used the breadfruit to supplement poi, which is made out of taro, in order to have more to eat. We simply ate whatever the land and sea offered, supplemented by what little we could afford to buy at the store.

One of the ways I made a little money was to go over to help out at the Hilo airport, which at that time didn't have a paved runway. Convicts maintained the grounds. I would help pump fuel from 55 gallon drums into the Army planes. I was paid a dime for that work. There were no civilian planes in those days.

There was a group of us who used to hang out by the wharf. We would sell coral to the tourists at the port, shine their shoes, and sell them newspapers for a nickel each. We would also scramble for money. We'd yell to the people on the ship to drop money on the pier and we would scramble for it. We'd dive after the money that fell in the water. If I made twenty-five cents, I considered myself lucky. That was a fun time in my life.

A year or two after we moved into our Homestead house in Keaukaha, my older brother Edwin moved in with my aunt and her family. A year later, he was diagnosed with Hanson's disease and immediately isolated in Hilo. Later, he moved to a compound in Honolulu. He never returned home.

My mother and her common-law husband lived together for many years and just before he died, they finally got married.

I was anxious to get away from my cramped living conditions and find my own way. I felt that the sooner I got a job and money, the sooner I would be able to choose where and how I wanted to live. I chose work over school and a new chapter in my life began.

THE SCHOOL OF HARD KNOCKS

In 1932 at 15 years of age, I decided to leave school and find work. I worked as a longshoreman, but it wasn't steady and I was always on the lookout for something better.

At the time, the Great Depression was affecting the whole world, including Hawaii. Jobs were hard to find. President Roosevelt started the Civilian Conservation Corps throughout the country to provide jobs for youth under the age of 20. The CCC was the first steady job that I had.

We worked on Mauna Kea at an elevation of six thousand feet. It was cold up there. Our job was to build a road around the mountain. Until then, the only way to get up was by horseback. It wasn't pleasant work, but we were provided a place to sleep, meals and thirty dollars a month. Twenty-five dollars went to my parents and I got to keep five dollars, but I didn't mind that.

We usually drank away the money we had left and because we were immature, we'd often get in fights. I grew tired of it all after a while and decided to leave after ten months.

I ended up back at the docks working as a longshoreman and moved into the housing close to work. Many ex-cons worked as longshoremen and lived there as well. A few of my friends worked there as well, but they lived at home. I liked my independence too much. I only saw my mother occasionally when I would ask her for some of the life insurance money that was sent due to my father's passing. She as never able to give much.

On payday, those of us who lived at the docks would go out and buy some beer and wine. That was our recreation. We often got drunk and would sometimes get into a little trouble, but it was usually minor.

Around the time I started as a longshoreman in 1933, a union man came over from the mainland to try to organize us. I lied about my age and applied to join. I was accepted and received membership card number twelve. I was officially a member of the International Longshoremen of America.

A lot of workers didn't want to sign up for the union, which caused conflict between union and non-union workers. I didn't agree with the techniques that unions used to harass and coerce those that didn't want to join.

There was a bar down by the waterfront and some of the longshoremen would point out guys that belonged to other unions. I was a little guy and some of the other members that we called bulls would have me go out and start trouble. I would go up to the targets and say something to aggravate them. They would go after me, but I wasn't that big so they wouldn't hit me. The bigger guys would back me up and beat up the ones I started talking to. I really didn't like being involved in this sort of thing.

Having reached the age of twenty, I was entitled to a lump sum payout from my father's accidental death insurance. I received one hundred dollars, which was quite a bit of money to me at the time. When I got word of the payment, I realized I had the chance to leave the environment I was in and decided right then to move on to something else.

I had been looking for something else to do and often saw sailors come in on boats. I thought it was something I might like. So, I joined the sailors union and received my card as a wiper. I bundled up my meager belongings and bought a ticket to Honolulu, hoping to ship from there. The price of my steerage class ticket was twelve dollars.

When I arrived in Honolulu in 1937, I didn't know anybody. The first thing I did was go to Union Hall hoping that I would ship out. I wasn't able to get a boat out right away and, before long, I met some people, including a young man by the name of Lloyd Wright. We drank together and he invited me to his family's property near Punchbowl. I stayed there in a little one-room shack separate from the family house.

I worked cleaning up schoolyards. The pay was poor, but it was enough for our booze. The job didn't last long. Eventually Momma Wright got fed up with my drinking and kicked me out of the house. I lived there for about one year. It was probably the best thing that could have happened to me, but it didn't seem that way at the time. I had no place to go.

When I left the Wright's house, I had a few belongings and eventually made my way to downtown Honolulu. On Hotel Street, I met some people that I knew and fell into their group. That's how I got to be a street person or bum.

We had a clique and our own territory to cover. We had a hierarchy of sorts and the Hotel Street gang was middle status. Everyone had a nickname; mine was Spider. Our daily routine was to panhandle and then we'd use that money to buy food and drinks. We'd sleep in vacant buildings or on park benches, or else we'd drink and pass out in the alleys.

During my time on the street, I spent numerous days in jail. In those days, if you staggered down the street, the police would put you in the wagon and haul you in. They'd lock you in the bullpen, which was one big jail room.

I never gave the police my real name; I made up the alias James Kealoha. I had relatives that lived in Honolulu and I didn't want the authorities to put my real name in print and hurt the family.

The longest jail sentence I had was three months. The good part about jail was that you could take a shower and put on clean clothes. Out on the street, we hardly ever took a bath. I was given two regular meals a day and a place to sleep. I was treated like a human being. Jail was monotonous though. You didn't have to do any work and there was nothing to do but read.

When you were finally released, you had no where to go but back on the street to the same old gang. They'd say, "Great to see you," and hand you a bottle, which is what got you into trouble in the first place.

I was informed somehow that I had a little money coming from my father's insurance and I had to go back to Hilo to collect it. The problem was that I didn't have any money to get to Hilo. One day, after drinking, I stowed away on a passenger ship headed to the Big Island.

In those days, you could get aboard a ship without a pass, but when you came off the boat, you had to show your ticket. A friend of mine on board gave me his ticket so I could disembark. A friend of his was on the ship's crew and let him into first class. He didn't have to show a ticket when he disembarked.

In Hilo, I found my way back on to the streets and into the jail routine. I met a couple of guys from Honolulu who were more or less street bums, like me. However, they were the leaders of the Bethel Street group in Honolulu. The Bethel Street group was a step up in status from the Hotel Street group, which I was previously part of.

A while later, my two friends and I decided to return to Honolulu. We stowed away on a boat to Maui for the big county fair and were able to catch a ride on a tugboat back to Honolulu.

Back in Honolulu, I stayed with my new friend Benny and his parents in a modest house and, of course, I was accepted into the Bethel Street gang. I had high status as far as the bums were concerned. While in the Bethel Street group, I didn't drink as heavy and didn't get arrested anymore. We were more respected and had more respect for ourselves. I met a lot of new people. Those people helped me then and later on after I left the street.

Now, when I look back, I think I reached bottom during my days on Hotel Street. My move to Bethel Street was my first step back up. My life on the street was an adventure. I survived and I learned a lot about life and about myself. Eventually, I got to a point where I felt I had outgrown that way of life.

FAMILY MATTERS

While I was on Bethel Street, I came to the conclusion that I needed a different aim in life. I wanted to do more than just hang out and panhandle.

I made a point to meet some of my father's cousins that were living in Honolulu. My dad's cousin had an influential position as superintendent of the wiring department with Hawaiian Electric. I asked him for a job and he was able to get me one as an apprentice electrician. It paid only thirty cents an hour, but it was the first regular job I had in years.

I worked regular hours during the week, learning under the journeyman electricians, and every Saturday I had to attend technical training classes. The idea was that eventually the apprentice would someday qualify for journeyman status. After a year, I graduated and was considered an apprentice helper.

After starting with Hawaiian Electric, I continued to live with Benny and his family for a while. I contributed part of my wages to the household, but the mother would often gamble it away. I was happy to find another place to live not long after starting work.

I made friends with Eddie Hore, another apprentice, and was invited to move in to his family home, which was in a nice neighborhood. I shared a bedroom with Eddie and we would often hit the bar route. His parents tolerated it, but they weren't very happy about it.

Living with the Hore family was an important step in improving my life. Prior to living with them, I had never sat down at a table and eaten a formal meal with a knife, fork and spoon in their proper places. I used to just grab a utensil and eat wherever, usually on the floor. I had to learn proper manners through observation. Here I was, twenty three years old and eating a proper meal for the first time in my life!

I was making thirteen dollars a week at the time; I contributed to household expenses and kept a few dollars for myself. I started to get involved with the family and made myself useful around the house.

Ed's parents took a liking to me and his father treated me like a son. Sometimes he would come by me when I was doing yard work and give me advice. He'd say, "Herbert, if you ever get married, try to get your own home before the wedding. If you can do that, you'll be way ahead." That advice stuck in my head.

When I moved out of Benny's house, he didn't blame me for wanting to find a better place. I remained friends with him and the rest of the Bethel Street gang. I'd see them out every now and again, and would often give them a little money or something to eat. We were all good friends.

Things seemed to be starting my way in life; however, the rest of the world was in turmoil.

"WE ARE AT WAR!"

I was happily settled in as an apprentice with Hawaiian Electric and had been living with the Hores for about a year when I was drafted into the Army in June 1941.

I took my basic training at Schofield Barracks and then was assigned to the Headquarters Company of the 298th Infantry Regiment, a former Guard unit that was federalized in 1940.

Toward the end of November 1941, people in Hawaii were aware that something was brewing, but no one had any idea what was going to happen. My unit was alerted to get into our designated positions and be prepared. Part of this preparation was drawing up our communication lines. We established observation points to look out on the horizon to see if there was anything coming in. We had our gun placements established as well. In other words, we were set in our defensive positions. Our unit was stationed on the windward side of the island.

On the weekend of the Japanese surprise attack on Pearl Harbor, I was off on a weekend pass. I was in Honolulu when the attack started early Sunday morning, December 7, 1941. We could hear the noise—the thumping sound—and when we looked out, we could see black smoke coming from the direction of Pearl Harbor. We were curious as to what was going on so we turned on the radio and heard the following announcement, "All military personnel report to your stations immediately! The Japanese have attacked

Pearl Harbor! We are at war! We repeat, all military personnel report to your stations immediately!"

My friend drove me down to the YMCA, which was the depot for military buses. I got on a bus with a bunch of others. We went to Schofield Barracks to get our things before heading out to our various posts. As the bus was passing above Pearl Harbor, I saw the whole thing. The attack was still going on and there was confusion everywhere. The USS *Arizona* was enveloped in flames; the USS *Oklahoma* was on its side. Those who had managed to escape from being trapped inside those ships were up on the hull, but the ocean was on fire from the spilled oil and fuel. Those men couldn't even go into the water. There was smoke all over and a lot of commotion.

As our bus arrived on Schofield Barracks, we passed Wheeler Field, the airfield where our fighter planes were kept. Our forces must have known something was going to happen because they had those planes lined up in a nice, straight row, ready to go. I guess they hadn't anticipated a sneak air assault. The Japanese attack was obviously well planned. They knew exactly what targets to hit. A group of their planes had flown directly to Wheeler Field and bombed our planes. Those planes were destroyed where they sat. I saw the destruction.

When we finally arrived at Schofield Barracks, we noticed that they had attacked the main barracks area, but not the wooden quarters where most of us were staying. We quickly got our stuff together, got in our trucks and went to our positions. When we were being trucked to our positions, we saw some enemy planes in the air, but they were a long way off from us.

On the way to the windward side of the island, we drove by Makapu Marine Base, which at that time was a Naval Air Station. They had patrol planes stationed in that area and I saw that those planes had been destroyed as well. Just as they had done at Wheeler, the Japanese caught all of those planes on the ground.

By the time I got into my position near Kailua at about 11am, the attack had been over for an hour or so. The Japanese planes had disappeared.

We were expecting the Japanese to follow up their air attack with an invasion. We got the machine gun unit out to the beach area and started to string barbwire. The invasion didn't happen. After that, every morning we were prepared. For six months, we were in a high alert situation.

I was a switchboard operator and because of that I got a lot of information from different positions and outposts. The day after the Pearl Harbor attack, I intercepted a message that a Japanese mini submarine had apparently lost its bearing and grounded off the beach in Waimanalo, which was close to where I was stationed. Troops from my regiment captured the survivor. That Japanese sailor was the first United States prisoner of war in World War II.

We later found out that there had been five mini subs launched against us. Their mission was to get into Pearl Harbor and sink our ships, but some of them got lost. None of them made it back to their mother ship. Of the five, one had managed to slip in and was detected at the entrance of Pearl Harbor. It was depth-charged just before the attack began. The other two subs just disappeared.

Our Regiment was responsible for covering and protecting the area between Makapuu Point and Waiahole, close to Chinaman's Hat. Our Regiment was one of several in our Division. After six months, they rotated or relieved our Regiment of that responsibility.

In the meantime, thousands of recruits were shipped over from the mainland. Hawaii became a training ground for the Marines and others, at first to guard against invasion and later to fight in the Pacific theater.

After our Regiment had been relieved of our duties guarding the windward shoreline, the military began pulling Japanese Americans out of our group, even though they were U.S. citizens. Many of the troops in my outfit were Japanese and because you can't visually tell the difference between a Japanese American and the enemy, the military felt the best strategy was to pull those troops and send them to the mainland. Once there, they were organized into the 442nd Regiment, which was later sent to fight the Germans in Europe.

Although it was not officially stated, the military decided to withdraw the Japanese American troops because they questioned their loyalty to the U.S. After all of that happened, I lost interest in the Regiment because many of my friends had been pulled out. I decided to apply for a transfer.

Since I had an electrical background, I thought I might qualify for the Signal Corps. On my next leave, I went to the Signal Corps headquarters to see if they needed any electricians. They said they could use me and they sent in a request for my transfer.

I was transferred to the Signal Corps at Fort Shafter in June of 1942. My job was to provide equipment to GIs serving in the Pacific. The 9th Signal Corps and the 220 Signal Corps both did the same job. I was part of the 220, which did more technical work.

The military began to see me as a person of ability and I was soon promoted. Before long, I was promoted to Staff Sergeant, which was about four ranks high. I was starting to really enjoy my progress. It gave me a sense of accomplishment and I wanted to improve myself further. The positions for non-commissioned officers were limited, however, and there weren't any vacancies that I could see.

If I wanted to advance, I had three options. I could apply to be an Aviation Cadet, Chief Warrant Officer or go to Officer's Cadet School. My dream was to be a pilot and, even though I hadn't finished tenth grade, I applied for a position as an Aviation Cadet in the Army Air Corps. There was no separate Air Force at the time. I was elated when my application was accepted.

KEESLER FIELD & CAMP SHELBY

In early 1944, I got orders to proceed to Keesler Field in Mississippi for training as an Aviation Cadet. I departed on a transport ship for the mainland on March 8, 1944, and arrived in Los Angeles on March 14. I stayed overnight on a base there and the following day boarded a train for Chicago.

I can't remember exactly how long I stayed in Chicago, but I was able to take in a little entertainment. Chicago was a good city for military personnel. We were able to get into almost anything without spending money. Our uniform granted us admission to most things. We went to the USO and they gave us tickets to the best shows—movies, stage shows, anything we wanted. The bus rides were free. Chicago really went all out for military personnel. When we went into a bar, the people would treat us to drinks. I had a little drinking bout there before catching the train to Keesler Field, which was located near Biloxi, Mississippi.

When I arrived at Keesler, I had a letter waiting for me from my Aunt Rose, who lived in Hilo on the Big Island. She explained that my Aunt Maud, my father's sister who lived in Iowa, was trying to contact me.

I wrote a letter to my Aunt Maud and explained that I would like to come and visit. I had not had leave since the Pearl Harbor attack outside of an overnight pass. As I hadn't started my new training yet, I thought that it was a good time to apply for extended leave. I was granted two weeks and decided to visit my long-lost relatives in Iowa.

I arrived at the Waterloo train station early in the morning where my cousin met me. We went to a coffee shop and my Aunt Maud came to meet us. We felt at home with one another and I stayed with them for a few days. After that, we always kept in contact.

I still had some furlough time left so I got back on the train and saw a bit more of the country. I eventually found my way down to New Orleans where I enjoyed a few days.

When I returned to Keesler, I had new orders. The military decided they didn't need any more Aviation Cadets at that time. They were planning to invade Europe and their priorities had changed. They needed more men in the infantry. I was transferred to the 69th Infantry Division at Camp Shelby in Mississippi. I was disappointed, but I wasn't the only one. A lot of us were in the same situation. We were all ranking non-commissioned officers with infantry background, and they needed experienced men to supervise all the new recruits being brought in to man the invasion force.

I reported to Camp Shelby in April of 1944. The 69th Division has been officially activated on May 15, 1943 and had been training at Camp Shelby since that time, awaiting further orders. The Division command assigned me to the 272nd Regiment, which is known as the Battleaxe Regiment. The 272nd attached me to the 2nd Battalion, Headquarters Company.

The Headquarters Company, which my Platoon was part of, was comprised of men that had special training or technical knowledge. While other Companies used rifles, we used our technical skills to contribute to their effort. We were specially trained to defuse explosives as well as supply explosives and other ammunition to our rifle companies. We were essentially the supply and support Company. The Headquarters Company assigned me to the Ammunition and Pioneers Platoon, known as the A&P.

I settled into training and around October 1, 1944, it became evident that my Regiment was going to be shipped overseas. On October 31, 1944, the Regiment left Camp Shelby for an unknown destination.

HELL ON EARTH

First, the Regiment traveled by train to Camp Kilmer in New Jersey, an overseas training area. Then, on November 14, 1944, the Regiment traveled by train and then ferry to two transport ships in New York Harbor. My battalion was put on a converted freighter, the SS *Santa Maria*. During the night of November 15, under the cover of darkness, two ships carrying the 272nd moved out of the harbor. The convoy, consisting of about 35 ships, assembled and began its trip across the Atlantic.

The voyage was actually fairly pleasant and on December 1, 1944, we docked at Southampton, England. We settled in camps nearby to await further orders. In the meantime, the Regiment was liberal with passes and I was able to visit London and other places.

The war seemed far away during the early part of December, until the newsflash of the German breakthrough in Belgium on December 16. After that, war seemed close at hand and our attitude changed from one of casual interest to one of serious personal regard. On Christmas day, seven hundred men were taken from the Regiment for immediate shipment to Belgium to help stop the German onslaught. It was about that time that the Regiment was warned to prepare for shipment to the battlefront.

On January 21, 1945, the Regiment sailed aboard the MS *Sobieski* through a blizzard from England to France. When we arrived offshore at Le Havre, we had to climb down a rope net ladder to our landing craft. When the craft hit the shore, they dropped the gate and we ran out onto the beach. Each man carried all of his belongings on his back in a duffel bag, including two sets of government-issued clothing, food supply, gas mask, sleeping bag, and half of a pup tent. Two men, each having half of a tent, would combine with another to make one tent. This was one way the Army encouraged teamwork.

The total weight of the duffel bag was about 80 pounds. In addition, we had to carry a rifle and heavy shoes. It was physically tough; we had to be in top shape. The infantry put us through rigorous training so that we could handle the physical demands that we would face.

I didn't really comprehend the horror of war until I saw the destruction in Le Havre, France. It was also my first experience with snow, real thick snow. It was beautiful, but cold.

After arriving on the beach at Le Havre, we proceeded by semi-trailer truck to a staging area. I can still vividly remember that truck ride. They packed us in like sardines; we couldn't move. Being tightly packed kept us a little warmer. I had never experienced cold like that before. We were all cold and uncomfortable.

The truck took us within the vicinity of Forges-Les-Eaux. Regimental Headquarters was located in Gaillefontaine with the battalions in the neighboring towns. The towns in this section of France had been ravaged by war, and the Regiment, for the most part, was quartered in ruined houses and old abandoned chateaux.

A group of us moved into an abandoned chateau. There was no heat or conveniences, but we made ourselves as comfortable as we could. The sleeping bags we carried with us were pretty snug. It was a narrow, mummy-type bag. We would climb in with our rifles, zip it up, and pull the top tight so that only our face was showing. We spent about a week in Forges-Les-Eaux.

On February 1, 1945, we moved by train to Laon, France. They put us in narrow boxcars. There was barely enough room to lie down. They put straw on the floor, but that was the only comfort as we rode across France. When it was time to eat, they would stop the train. We'd get out and light our little can of fuel, which we used to heat our food. That train trip was long, tiresome and cold.

When we arrived near Laon, we settled in the surrounding towns, but by February 6, we were on the move again by train to Born, Belgium. The trip was two days and two nights, and seemed even rougher than the previous. At Born, the Regiment was placed in V Corps, a part of the First United States Army.

On February 12, 1945, we moved from Born to the front. The Division replaced the 99 Infantry Division in the Eifel Forest area. The 272nd Infantry was placed in V Corps reserve and was located in the forest near Losheinergraben.

The whole area was part of the German bulge. It was littered with destroyed or abandoned German equipment and the bodies of dead animals and Germans. The area was within light artillery range and the enemy strafed our position on several occasions. The weather was still extremely cold and the snow melted just enough to make the ground muddy.

The conditions were miserable. We settled in one spot for a time, entrenched, and then secured the territory just taken from the enemy. This is known as bivouacking. Then we would wait until the right time to move against the famous Siegfried line.

The Siegfried Line was an impressive line of defense that the Germans had built out of concrete obstacles that many likened to "dragon teeth." These obstacles were intended to stop tanks and other vehicles from trying to cross into Germany. The Line was built along the western border of Germany, stretching 1,000 miles to the North Sea.

Artillery was firing over our heads. All we had for shelter was our pup tents. We were in between the German guns and our own. If a shell from the Germans fell short of its target, it would have blown us up. For extra protection from shelling, we dug a hole in the muddy ground to put our tent into. Despite the cold, we couldn't have a fire because the smoke would give away our position.

Our clothes were wet and dirty, but our feet were our biggest problem. They were constantly damp and we didn't have access to clean, dry socks. Many of us developed "trench foot," because our feet were never dry and couldn't heal. I developed terrible sores all over my feet and between my toes. The medics gave me tincture of iodine to put on my feet, but it only relieved the itching. This was the worst part of the whole thing. It was uncomfortable, painful and frustrating.

As a non-commissioned officer, my duty was to look after my men before myself. I had to distribute rations and assign men to guard duty. These things weren't enjoyable, as I had to do them under very trying conditions.

The Germans were trying to hold back our forces from entering their country. They fired heavy artillery and strafed us with their planes. The sound of strafing was like 1,000 stampeding horses. You don't know where the plane is coming from, but when the bullets come down, you can hear them hitting the ground. It was a terrible stress. You never knew from one minute to the next if you were going to be killed.

With all of the cold, filth and discomfort, life was unbearable. After a while, I got so down that I would deliberately stick my leg out when I dove for cover, hoping to get hit in the leg and sent to the hospital. Many men did the same. Now, I'm thankful that didn't happen.

We were entrenched in that area for what seemed like forever, but it was actually only a little more than two weeks. On February 27, the 69th Division attacked the Siegfried Line. On March 1, 1945, the 272nd Regiment relieved the 273rd Regiment and assumed a front line position. We were finally leaving our hell in the Eifel Forest. Whatever lay ahead had to be better.

As we penetrated the line and moved into Germany, we had to clear the roads of mines so that the rest of the convoy could move ahead. The road mines were larger anti-tank or anti-vehicular and had to be run over to be set off. Most of the off-road mines were anti-personnel and designed so that a single man could trip the device. The Germans put up signs indicating the location of the mines so their own men wouldn't be killed. They were in such a rush when they retreated that they didn't have time to take down the signs!

Anti-personnel mines could be easily cleared, but the mine itself could be booby-trapped so we had to be careful. We would get a long line with a hook and attach it to the mine. We would move about 50 yards away before yanking the whole thing out of the ground. If nothing exploded, you would pick up the mine and set it aside to be defused later on.

Working with the mines wasn't all that dangerous because we knew how they were triggered. Dealing with them became a matter of routine. The only time it was really dangerous was in the beginning when we were just learning.

When our platoon stopped, I would line my men up and order them to get out their trenching tools and clean up the area. The Germans didn't dig a trench for their waste and the men would have to scrape it up and bury it.

After the site was cleaned, we would bivouac. It was usually a short stay because we had to keep up with the front. General Patton and his tanks were clearing the way ahead and we moved as fast as the front line infantry was able to push forward. The Germans were firing at us as we moved.

If we were expected to be under enemy fire, we'd unload all of the ammunition and equipment from the trucks and move it a safe distance away. When we were ready, we'd load it back up again. It was a heavy job for us.

During the war, you had to try to see the humor in things. One day, a hot meal truck came in. It was a big treat and we all rushed to line up to get hot food. While in line, the Germans started strafing us. The men scattered from the food truck. We dove under cover and took shelter on the opposite side of big trees. As soon as the noise of the plane was gone, everyone dashed back to the chow wagon as fast as possible in order to get a better place in line! I thought that was kind of comical. We had hot meals as often as possible, but we couldn't have them everyday. A hot meal was a treat and they helped keep morale high amongst the troops.

As we moved forward, we were led by the infantry rifle Companies. When the German tanks blocked the way, our tanks would be called forward to fight them.

One of our jobs was to destroy all of the German anti-tank guns. We would pile ammunition around the guns and blow them up. This was to ensure that even if the Germans executed a counter attack and recovered their position, they would not be able to use those guns against us. The engineers would then come in after us and use blowtorches to cut the gun barrels.

Sometimes we would encounter big German ammunition dumps or storage areas. We'd haul those mines and other enemy ammunition out to a farmer's field and blow the whole bunch up. The poor famers would get mad at us because the blast would destroy the farmland, but we considered it an important job and thought we were doing a greater good.

When we went into most of the towns, all you saw was rubble. Our bombers, artillery and tanks would totally destroy everything before we got there. The civilians would go underground and into cellars during the bombing. I spoke to many of those German people and, in fact, many of the younger generation spoke some English.

As we advanced further into Germany, we came upon a number of labor camps. When we opened the doors to those places and freed the people, they just went crazy with joy and excitement. I witnessed the liberation of a number of those labor camps during the latter stages of the way. I was witness to the fact that many of the people in the labor camps weren't treated well. They were undernourished and lived in clapboard buildings. Many became ill and died.

We finally met up with the Russians at Torgau on the Elbe River towards the end of April 1945. At that point, our part of combat was essentially complete. It wasn't necessary for us to advance any further because the Russians had reached the Berlin area, which they wanted to capture in order to secure the surrender of Germany. We started to withdraw and the Russians took over some of the territory that we had at that point.

Our Company withdrew to the village of Hohenmuellsen. We settled in and awaited further orders. Around that time, we got word that President Roosevelt had died. Then on May 8, 1945, it was announced that Germany had surrendered. The war in Europe was over!

During my time in Hohenmuellsen, I met a German girl. It was an interesting relationship because she couldn't speak English and I couldn't speak German. We had a little book issued to us by the Army with German words and phrases in it. That was the extent of our communication. Nevertheless, we got quite attached. Her father was a Swiss citizen so I encouraged her and her parents to return to Switzerland, which they eventually did.

Our communication was serious and I planned to eventually have her join me in America, but after about a year the relationship fizzled out.

Our unit eventually occupied the town of Bad Ems and while we were there, I got into some trouble. I remember going out with the other troops and having cognacs in the hotel. Then, a Sergeant and I picked up a bicycle outside of the hotel. He rode on the handlebars and I was pedaling. We went to a German home and I must have asked them for a drink. I don't remember anything after that, but when I woke up, I was locked in a German prison.

My Company Captain told me that he would represent me at my hearing and he was confident that he could clear things up. However, that next weekend, I got in trouble again. After that, my Captain decided not to represent me. I was immediately removed from my responsibilities after I was charged, but I kept my rank and pay pending the outcome of the court hearing. I didn't face my court martial until after we withdrew our forces and Germany surrendered. I plead guilty and they took away my stripes and moved me back to the rank of Private.

This was an embarrassing situation for me, but it was good that it happened. It forced me to face up to certain things.

After the war in Europe ended, we went from being a combat force to being an occupation force. I remained stationed in Germany. We didn't have much work to do as occupation troops so they tried to keep us busy. One of the activities they offered was boxing so I joined the team. I thought I might as well give it a shot.

Soon afterward I was transferred from the 69th Infantry Division to the 29th Infantry. Their headquarters was in Bremen. From there, I went to Breminhoffen to train for boxing.

In the summer of 1945, the United States began to prepare for redeployment of many of our troops to the Pacific theater. Not long after the talk started, we got word in August 1945 that Japan had surrendered. Word came in September that I was eligible for discharge.

In the days and weeks after the end of the war, I reflected on my experiences during the approximately three months I was in combat.

Although I didn't cause any death by my own hand, I saw a lot of it. It was shocking at first, but we eventually developed a morbid sense of humor about it. It was our way of coping with tragedy. I still remember seeing dead soldiers laying about when I first arrived at the Eiffel Forest. I thank God that it wasn't my primary job to kill people. It would have weighed heavily on my mind.

In the infantry, you don't see everything; you don't see the big picture. News didn't get around very quickly. All you care about is your orders for that day, what you personally have to deal with. You find out all of these other things after the war and only then do you get a full picture of what happened. It was only through reading the Regiment book that I found out about most of the things that had gone on within my own Regiment!

The sores on my feet took a long time to heal and more than 50 years later, I don't have much feeling in them. It took me a while to break the habit of swearing so much. Combat has a profound effect on the way you talk. Whenever I heard a loud noise, I would dive for cover. It took me a long time to get that out of my mind.

It was a good thing that I had a little break after combat and before being discharged. It gave me a chance to get my mind back in order again and to more readily adjust to civilian life. The time that I spent boxing gave me a chance to get away from the war. I was more or less adjusted by the time I got home.

I'm glad that I had that combat experience, but I wouldn't wish it on another human being. I was drafted and I didn't have any other choice, but, given the chance, I probably would have enlisted anyway.

I left my post in Germany on October 1, 1945 and proceeded to my designated port at Antwerp, Belgium, where I boarded a ship for the U.S. We landed in Boston and I was ordered to travel across country by train to an Army camp in California. I reported to camp on October 14, 1945.

For the first time since leaving the Hawaiian Islands in 1944, I heard Pidgin English and my ears perked up. Some boys from the 442nd were there and, like me, they were about to be discharged and would be going home to Hawaii. It was strange hearing Pidgin English after such a long time. It brought on a little feeling of homesickness.

MAKING MY WAY

I was stationed in California for about one month. Finally, on December 1, 1945, I boarded a ship bound for Hawaii. The trip took one week and I arrived in Honolulu on December 7, 1945, exactly four years to the day since the Japanese attack on Pearl Harbor.

I had not been discharged from the Army so when I arrived in port I was required to report to Fort Kamehameha to await my formal discharge. On December 10, 1945, I received my honorable discharge along with one hundred dollars of the total three hundred dollars in mustering out pay that I was eligible for. I went back to live with the Hore family.

Eddie Hore had volunteered for the Navy and was assigned to Pearl Harbor patrol. He was there for the whole war. He was never sent into combat. Eddie and I were discharged at the same time, but before going back to work, we decided to take some R&R. We took a trip to the Big Island and had a rip-roaring good time. After about a month, we were relaxed and ready to go back to work.

We both went back to our jobs as apprentice electricians at Hawaiian Electric, but there didn't seem to be any sign of advancement for us there. Later, we both got offers to work at the Navy Yard in their electrical shop, which paid more than double what we were paid at Hawaiian Electric. At Hawaiian Electric, we earned our money. At the Navy Yard, they had to find jobs to keep us busy. There was no job satisfaction.

I decided to get in contact with Leo Pritchard, the man I worked for when I was in the Signal Corps. He held a high civilian position in the Signal Corps at Fort Shafter. He was able to get me a job with a little more pay. Before long, however, I decided it was time to get more education.

I decided I would like to go to university to become an electrical engineer. Although I hadn't completed 12th grade, they gave veterans a break. If we could pass the university entrance exam, we would be accepted. My Aunt Maud suggested that I attend the University of Iowa and stay with her while I was in school.

I only attended the University of Iowa for one semester. I soon realized that my previous lack of education was too much of a handicap to overcome. I had been away from regular school for more than thirteen years!

A vocational school seemed like a better alternative so I transferred to Coyne Electrical School in Chicago. The government paid my tuition through the GI Bill. The course taught me the practical application of electrical and gave me the classroom qualification for my journeyman's papers. It also gave me an advantage over others looking for jobs; I never had trouble getting a job after that.

While my time at University of Iowa was short lived, I got to experience college life, including dorm life and how to study. I also took a communications skills class that taught me proper English, including public speaking techniques.

When I returned to Hawaii, Hawaiian Electric hired me to work in their wiring department. The department was eventually done away with and Hawaiian Dredging Company, the same company that my father worked for, hired me.

Hawaiian Dredging had just acquired a floating dry dock from the Navy and they hired me to work on it. A dry dock is a big piece of machinery that extends about 200 feet in length. It's made of concrete and picks up the ships that float into it so that repairs can be made on the parts of the ship that are normally under water. The ship floats into the dry dock and then they pump the water out and raise the ship up and place it on blocks.

With a crew under me, I was in charge of operating and maintaining all of the electrical equipment aboard the unit. I learned as I was doing the job. It was challenging and I enjoyed it. During that time, I also met a very special person.

LEHUA CHRISTINA LEE LOY

During the time I was working on the drydock, I was still living with Eddie and his family. I was doing a lot of partying, not really saving any money, and I had no real goals. That changed in 1948 when I met Lehua.

After the war, my mother used to come to Oahu from Hilo and we'd take a plane to Kalaupapa on the island of Molokai to visit my brother. On one particular visit, my aunt accompanied us. After we returned from Molokai, I dropped my mother and aunt off at my aunt's house, but I didn't go in myself. I went home and got cleaned up and was planning to go to the movies. For some reason, I decided to go back to my aunt's house.

When I arrived at my aunt's house, I noticed a pretty girl by the door. Something attracted me to her right away and I said, "Hello." I recognized her as a girl that I had known years before when we were both much younger. I used to play with her brothers when we all lived in the same neighborhood in Hilo. She didn't seem to remember me. I had no girlfriend at the time, so I asked, "Are you married?"

She answered, "No, but I'm looking."

And I replied, "I'm available."

We knew right then we were right for each other. We didn't play any games and got straight to the point. She had a date with someone else that night, but she didn't keep it. She spent the evening with me and later I took her home. We went through a courtship period.

Lehua later told me that earlier that day she had been to church. She prayed to either meet someone nice or to open a beauty shop. She had gone to beauty school in Seattle and was working for a little shop in Honolulu. In any event, it was meant to be. The timing was perfect.

Lehua didn't remember me from Hilo, but I remembered her. I am nine years older than her and she was just a little girl at the time. When I was staying with my Aunt Rose in Hilo, Lehua and her family lived on the same street.

The day I met Lehua, I stopped drinking. Since she didn't remember me from before, she didn't know I had been a drinker. Her father and her family remembered me and knew about my days as a bum in Hilo. I didn't have a very good reputation in Hilo, which was a small town at the time.

We courted for a couple of years, but I knew her parents didn't approve of me. We didn't have enough money to get married and I certainly didn't have enough to buy a home, as Mr. Hore had advised me. I didn't touch alcohol during all this time. I was determined to do right by Lehua.

As time went by, Lehua's parents saw that I wasn't drinking and slowly came around. They realized I was sincere and that I would maybe make a good husband for their daughter. I think in the back of their minds, they were still a little concerned.

During the time Lehua and I were courting, I was transferred within Hawaiian Dredging to work on a dredging machine in Pearl Harbor. In the fall of 1950, Hawaiian Dredging received a government contract to dredge Kwajalein Atoll in the Marshall Islands. It was a chance for me to make some extra money and maybe save enough to buy a house.

When I first saw Kwajalein, I was shocked at the devastation. It had been flattened during the war. The Japanese had a stronghold there and U.S. troops invaded the island. The artillery fire flattened everything. The coconut trees were wiped out; there was only one tree standing. Almost every Japanese soldier was killed, thousands of them.

The dredge I worked on was about 200 feet long with a large diesel engine that was converted to electrical. The dredge was a self-contained unit, equipped with a pump in the front and a cutter, which dug up coral from the ocean floor. The pump sucked stuff up and threw it about two miles off. It was like a giant vacuum cleaner. It was my responsibility to ensure the motor operated properly and was in good condition.

The dredge broke down after about four months. Luckily, our portion of the job was finished. We used the Navy's floating drydock to pick up the dredge and bring it back to Pearl Harbor for repairs.

I made pretty good money in Kwajalein. Our lodging and food was provided so when I got paid, I kept $5 and sent the rest home. There was a lot of gambling going on and sometimes I would win as much as $150 or $200 off of my measly $5. I sent the extra money home. In the four months I was there, I was able to save more than $3,000.

In the meantime, I had written and asked a good friend to propose to Lehua for me. I even sent him money to buy a ring. He gave her the ring and said the words I had asked him to on my behalf. She accepted! I guess you could call it a proposal by proxy. When I got back from Kwajalein, we set the date to get married. We settled for June 2, the day before my birthday.

About one month before our wedding, we found a nice home priced at only $10,000. We started the buying process and had all the paperwork finalized two weeks before we got married. We put $1,000 down. The people who were selling it were moving to the mainland. They sold us everything.

We were married June 2, 1951 at St. Theresa Catholic Church in the Palama area of Honolulu. It was a nice wedding, but, like everyone else, I had a few toasts. Just like that, I was a drinker again.

THE PHILIPPINES

I didn't go off the wagon immediately after the wedding, but that toast was just enough for me to start drinking again. As we settled into our home life, I gradually increased the amount I drank.

Six months after we got married, I went on the dredge to the Philippines. Lehua and I had gotten into an argument before I left and weren't on speaking terms. I had been drinking and went to buy a Zenith radio because I wanted to keep up with the news on the Korean War on the dredge. It was $60, which was a lot of money back then. Lehua was mad I had spent so much on it.

I was expected to be away on the dredge for several months. I would have preferred to stay in Pearl Harbor. It saddened me to be away from Lehua for so long and I departed for the Philippines with mixed feelings.

With the drydock in tow, we busied ourselves by working on the dredge. Work needed to be done to ensure that it would operate properly when we arrived. We lived right on the dredge and the Navy crew lived on the drydock. They even had a movie theater. Sometimes in the evening when our work was done, we'd get off the dredge, go up the gangway, and enjoy a movie or some other recreation. We were at sea for a whole month before we saw land. It was a long, slow adventure.

We arrived at Subic Bay in the Philippines in early 1952. The Navy Engineers or Sea Bees supervised the project. The goals were to dredge out the harbor to allow for easier docking and larger ships, and to improve and extend the airplane runway. After the end of the war, the U.S. tried to better secure Allied positions in the Philippines. With the Korean War underway, this became a priority. The Navy was in a hurry to get the harbor and the runway finished as soon as possible.

I had a group of men working under me and I had to instruct them on how to properly operate all of the electrical motors and pumps on the dredge. It was a tricky process and we had to do a trial run to figure out how it all worked. We dredged the material from one area, thereby deepening and widening the harbor, and piped it to where it was needed to build the runway. In this way, our dredge served a double purpose.

The project was a good experience because it was more like an engineering project. You had to solve electrical and mechanical problems, and sometimes you had to be creative about it. The drawback was that the whole crew drank.

Lehua and I didn't speak the whole time I was at sea. Even after I arrived in the Philippines, we didn't speak for some time. I got word somehow that Lehua had been carrying twins and that she had miscarried. I hadn't even known she was pregnant! I felt bad. We eventually started to communicate again and when my four-month contract was up, I happily flew home.

When I got back, we settled into home life again, but my drinking continued. I was a little uncomfortable at home now and missed work. I asked Hawaiian Dredging if they needed me in the Philippines. They did, so I went back.

When I got back to the Philippines, there was a major problem with the dredge. A rock got stuck in the line and burned out the electric motor. The dredge was inoperable and needed to be repaired. The longer it sat idle, the more money Hawaiian Dredging was losing. I volunteered to do the repair.

We worked day and night on the thing and were able to get it running in only ten days! The Navy engineers estimated that it would take much longer. I think that was a feather in my cap.

I worked on the dredge for six months, maybe a little longer. It was some of the most interesting work I did. It was a challenge and very satisfying. Eventually, however, I decided that it wasn't right for me to be away from Lehua for so long. I decided to leave and return home.

When I got back from the Philippines, Hawaiian Dredging didn't have a position open for me on Oahu at that time. I gave some serious thought to starting my own electrical business. Lehua and I knew it was a risk, but we felt that it was a risk worth taking.

WEATHERWAX ELECTRIC

In early 1953, Kailua was a growing community with a population of about 600. I started my business with a four-door sedan and stored my equipment and materials in the back.

Learning how to be a businessman was not an easy matter. I went to see my friend Leo Pritchard for advice. He suggested that I print up some one-cent postcards to mail out to people in the community. I included my business name and my slogan—If you have any problems, relax, call Weatherwax. I mailed out 100 and kept 200 to hand out or mail later.

Requests for work started to come in and, before long, I had enough work to keep me busy. Owning a business was a learning process. I needed to learn how to keep records, pay business taxes and all that. Lehua helped me with phone calls sometimes, but, for the most part, I wanted to keep her away from it so she wasn't concerned with business matters. I was operating out of my home, which I did not have the proper authority to do.

Not long after I started the business, I met Joe Correa, a plumber. He was also operating out of his home and suggested that we find a place together to carry out our business. We found a small place in Kailua owned by a contractor. We rented a shack to run our businesses out of for twenty five dollars a month. We had our own desks and shared a phone. I think we had one of the first answering machines. We got a kick out of playing with that thing.

Joe and I liked to have a few drinks, even at work. Before you know it, we would forget about our jobs and let the machine answer our calls. In time, we had workers with us who liked to drink too. Joe's wife would come around and we would hide whatever we were drinking. Lehua suspected that something was going on, but didn't bother to come around.

It was not really a happy time as far as family life was concerned. It was one of those periods that we went through and thank goodness we came out of it. We survived and the business survived as well.

I never had a lot of people working for me at one time, but I did hire quite a number over the years. The answering machine was our first secretary and my daughter Mary Elizabeth worked for me after I moved the business to a new office in the 1960s. Helen Correa (no relation to Joe) worked for me for many years and we became good friends.

As the amount of work increased, I started to hire service people to go out on calls. There was a time when I had about five electricians working for me as well as a couple of trucks on the road.

During the 1960s, I ran for political office and I formed a corporation for the electrical business. A good friend who had been working for me invested five thousand dollars in the corporation and received a small percentage of the shares. He was also my political campaign manager.

During the time I was politicking, I was away from my job a lot. A few of my employees pulled me aside and let me know they thought my friend was stealing from me. I investigated and found out it was true. I confronted him and he agreed to forfeit his share of the company because he knew I could charge him with fraud. He was caught and had no argument.

Those were some of the things that happened at Weatherwax Electric over the years.

"GOD, HELP ME!"

For a long time time, I knew that something was not going right with my life. I wasn't coming home to my family on time and when I did arrive, I was usually inebriated.

One such evening in 1955 was typical. I had gone out with the boys and got home late. Lehua was waiting for me at the door with a smile on her face. I knew she could tell I had been drinking. My eyes always got glassy when I drank.

After I got into the house, I fell on my knees in the bedroom and began to cry, "God, help me." I realized that I had a problem. I asked Lehua to call Alcoholic Anonymous for me. She called the number and a man answered the phone. He came to my home and explained what AA was all about. He invited me to the next AA meeting.

I had first heard about AA from the Hollywood movie "The Lost Weekend" and heard that it also existed in Hawaii. I didn't know much about the program, but I knew they helped individuals like me.

On an early Sunday morning, Lehua, our baby Mary Elizabeth, and I went to my first AA meeting. That was more than 42 years ago. I have not had a single drink of alcohol since. I'm happy to say that none of my children ever saw their papa take a drink of alcohol.

I had never talked about joining AA or even quitting before that day. Lehua and I had never discussed it. She never told me that I had a problem, but she obviously knew. She later told me that she had asked the Benedictine Sisters to pray for me and that she had been praying for me at St. Anthony's Church. Maybe all that praying contributed to what happened.

It took me a while to get over drinking. I was on edge for a long time and could not stand still. I reacted differently to things. After a while, I was able to break the pattern of going to the bottle whenever I had a problem. Instead, I would go down to the beach and read the paper.

It was a difficult transition period and it took years for me to fully separate from the dependency. I believe what made the difference is that I immediately latched on to the AA program. I got involved helping others right from the start. I took calls in the central office and volunteered to go out to homes when people called for help.

I can't say enough about what the AA program has meant to me. It is more than just a way to stop drinking; it provides guidelines that can be used to deal with almost anything you may confront in life.

KAILUA HOME SERVICE, INC.

Around 1960, my business partner Joe Correa learned they were going to open a semi-industrial development in our area. Joe started asking other business in the vicinity if anyone was interested in applying for one of those plots of land from the developer.

He approached me, but I didn't have the money. I thought that maybe we could borrow some from the bank. I talked to Lehua about it and she wasn't too keen on the idea. Joe's wife didn't want anything to do with the whole thing either.

I don't remember how it transpired, but we got a loan at the bank and I used my house for collateral. Joe and I formed a corporation and each put down five thousand dollars toward purchasing the lease in the new development. We decided to name our corporation Kailua Home Service, Incorporated.

We had a fifteen-thousand-square-foot business lot and a fifty-year lease on the property that expired in 2010. We picked out a corner plot, but couldn't put a building up right away because we didn't have the money. We got another loan from the bank and were able to put up a two unit, concrete building.

We were going to use the building for our businesses, but we eventually decided to lease it out and operate our businesses out of the same old shack we had been in for years. We were paying cheap rent and we were able to get enough from leasing the new units to cover the mortgage payments on the bank loan. Our investment was paying for itself.

Even after we put up that big building, there was still an unused space at the front of the property. Joe and I decided to put a putting green in there to occupy the land until we could afford to build more. We thought we could charge people to use it and maybe generate a little income from the unused space.

Joe and I had lots of energy, and with a little help from our friends, we built the putting green ourselves. The groundskeeper from the golf course at Kaneohe Marine Corps Air Station taught us how to plant the grass in just the right way. It really turned out well and we took pride in it. We had seven holes in it and even had floodlights that shone down for night use.

The problem was we never did have enough people use it. We were at the end of the development and had hardly any traffic going by. Joe and I would practice out there and have people come around to play, but the demand wasn't great enough to continue utilizing the space.

We eventually built three more units and relocated our own businesses from that old shack. They were a little smaller than the first two units. The putting green became a parking area. Joe moved his plumbing business into one unit and I moved into another. Weatherwax Electric has been there ever since.

Joe and I reached the age of sixty five in 1982 and we both retired. We figured that we were eligible for our Social Security and maybe we didn't have to go out anymore and break our necks. Sadly, Joe was killed in an accident a few years ago. His heirs own 50 percent stock in the corporation.

In the meantime, our jointly owned corporation, which owns the original property, still goes on. The building is still in good shape and will probably last one hundred years. Weatherwax Electric (owned by my son), an Elks Lodge, an espresso bar, hairdresser and clothing store occupy the units. A freestanding shave ice unit is also located on the property.

The plot of land and the building that Joe and I put up was an excellent investment. We used to sit down together and count our blessings. We would say to each other that it was the best investment we ever made.

Our lease expired in 2012 when I was ninety three years old. I worked out an arrangement whereby I passed on my fifty percent interest to my children. It is theirs to negotiate with the landlord.

EDDIE

My brother Eddie and I didn't live together very long. Our family couldn't afford to give us many things and he left home when I was about eleven to live with my Aunt Rose and her family. However, even in the years before he moved out, we did not have a strong connection. He was two years older and he never wanted to associate with me. I guess he considered me to be mostly a nuisance. I wanted to accompany him and would try to follow, but he'd throw rocks at me and keep me back. I laugh about it now, but that was how our relationship was back then.

Eddie was popular when he went to school. His classmates liked him and because he was a nice-looking young man, he attracted the girls. All of that changed suddenly when he was just fifteen years old. The day he was diagnosed with Hansen's Disease (formerly known as leprosy), his whole world changed virtually overnight. In those days there was no cure or vaccine for the dreaded affliction. Hansen's Disease was thought to be extremely contagious and as soon as someone was known to have it, they were immediately isolated.

So it was with Eddie. He was immediately put in quarantine in a facility in Hilo and, a short while later, was shipped over to Honolulu to Kalihi Settlement, which was specifically set up for people who suffered from the disease. It was in many ways like a prison. It was fenced in to keep the patients and general public from mixing. He was there for two years before finally being moved over to the more humane isolation settlement of Kalaupapa on Molokai. There, with the exception of a few shorts stays in hospitals in Honolulu, he lived out the rest of his life.

My mother stayed in contact with Eddie through letters but because the two of us hadn't been close prior to his illness, we fell out of contact. I did think about him once in a while and my mother mentioned him now and again, but I was not in contact with her much either.

By 1939, when I decided to try and see him, we had not communicated since he was shipped over to Honolulu in 1930. I was still panhandling on the streets of Honolulu in 1939 when I managed to get free passage on a boat to Molokai. When I arrived, I hitchhiked up the Pali (cliff) overlooking Kalaupapa. From the top of the Pali, you had to go down a trail to get to the settlement. Because of its location—encircled by the Pali on one side and the ocean on the other—the settlement is totally isolated. To this day, there is no other way to get there by land except to go down the trail. You can go down by mule or you can hike down as I had to. The trail is steep so you have to be careful that you don't miscalculate your step and topple over the cliff.

When I arrived at the bottom of the trail that day and came across some of the patients, their deformed faces startled me. It was a complete shock to see what the disease did to people. The patients I met had a guttural voice because their voice box was affected by the disease. After we greeted one another, I explained, "I'm here to visit Edwin Weatherwax." And they replied, "Oh yeah, Weatherwax, he's down there." So, I continued on in the direction they had pointed.

When I found my brother, I discovered that his voice had already been affected and he had the same gravelly tone. We were happy to see each other again after such a long separation and we had a pleasant time catching up on things. I stayed only one day before climbing back up the trail and into the so-called "normal" world. Before I left, he gave me something. At the time, you must remember, I was flat broke and being a smoker I could always use a few cigarettes. Knowing this, when I left that day, my brother gifted to me a carton of Camel cigarettes to take with me. It seems such a small thing now, but at that time it meant a lot to me and I never forgot it.

Circumstances saw to it that I didn't get to see Eddie again until after the war. I used to fly over there with my mother to visit every now and again. After my mother died, I continued to visit, albeit not often, so that he would know that I was still around and that I cared. Although, I have to admit that he had to remind me that I should come visit every once in a while.

Kalaupapa always had an airstrip, but it was not very long and could only handle small planes like the Beechcraft that we flew in on and made regular flights to Molokai. Those who visited usually stayed overnight, as I always did. They had facilities for visitors. In most settlements, the patients were isolated, but at Kalaupapa the patients had the run of the place and the visitors were isolated. They had a little visiting area. That was the way it was.

Thankfully, in later years, they were able to change that policy when they found out that Hansen's Disease isn't that contagious and a vaccine was developed for those who exhibited any signs of the disease. If it was caught early enough, the vaccine would stop its progress and make you immune to it. So, as a result of that advance, they could then safely allow visitors to intermingle. I never needed the vaccine myself.

In later years, Eddie was brought over to Honolulu now and again for treatments and medical testing. They had a hospital on Kalaupapa, but they were conducting tests in Honolulu on those who had an advanced stage of the disease. By then the damage to Eddie's physical body was too far advanced for treatments to make much of a difference. His hands and fingers were shrunk and deformed. Eddie was a guinea pig, in a medical sense. He agreed to be experimented on, if not to help himself, then to help others.

Towards the end, when I visited him in Kalaupapa, he was hospitalized and had his own room. They had operated on him to remove his eyeballs, which had been affected by the disease, and he was totally blind. Since that happened, his sense of hearing became pretty sharp. He could hear footsteps and know who was coming. One time, I went to visit him and didn't tell him I was coming. I was walking towards his room and all of sudden I heard him yell out, "Herbert! How the hell are you?" That made me smile.

When I visited, we'd talk and despite his unfortunate circumstances he had a good sense of humor and philosophy. I gained a lot from him by observing what he had to go through. It made me appreciate what I had. Despite his affliction, he never seemed despondent or depressed. He gave me the impression that he was living each day as best he could. I began to count my blessings. I knew that it could just as easily have been me. Why he got it and not me, no one will ever know. Realizing that fact gave me the fortitude to carry on and realize how fortunate I was in comparison to other people. I realized that I should be more grateful for what I had. My experiences with my brother made a big difference on my outlook on life. In this way, something tragic benefitted me by making me appreciate things more.

When I first started visiting my brother, he admitted that in the beginning he was really upset about his diagnosis. No one can accept that sort of thing in the beginning. He told me that he used to drink a lot and, as a result, was often in trouble in the Kalaupapa community. Kalaupapa is similar in many ways to any outside community. It has individuals who drink and raise hell and a police force to deal with them. He said that he eventually straightened up, stopped drinking, and began to get along in life.

One day in 1965, when he was already having all kinds of complications, he was brought to a special unit they had for Hansen's Disease patients at The Queen's Medical Center. I went to visit him and again was reminded of how fortunate I was. He was in bad shape, with all kinds of tubes and such things hooked up to him. Nevertheless, he seemed to have a good attitude. That was the last time I saw him. They took him back to Kalaupapa where, not long after, he passed on at the relatively young age of 50.

They say he died of natural causes, but specifically he died from liver failure. They say people don't actually die from Hansen's Disease, but it is a factor. Eddie drank heavily to try to drown his sorrows and eventually developed liver problems as a result. In that sense, the disease is never the direct cause of death.

Eddie and I never really had what you could call a close relationship, but we were blood brothers and in the end that is what bonded us together. I've never forgotten him or the lessons I learned through him. He is now entombed in the same vault with my father's urn at Oahu cemetery.

GOING OUT & DOING IT

I ran for the Hawaii House of Representatives in the 1966 election, although my initial intention was to run for city council. There was a lot of turmoil going on when we had the hippie movement out here and some things upset me. I thought to myself, "Why don't I try to do something about it." I was inspired to run for public office not knowing the expenses I'd run in to.

Like almost everything in life that I went through, I went into politics blind. I didn't go out and get surveys done or anything else of that nature. My approach was simple. I had something that I felt should be done and I did it! The officials told me what I had to do and I did it. I got so many signatures and went down to register. Then you put in some sort of agreement and you start campaigning.

To start with I was bipartisan. My aim was for a particular thing and I didn't care what party I was involved in. But then I met someone who advised me to join a certain party and they would help me get elected. I ended up running as a Democrat, which I think was the right move. I'm glad I had the experience of politicking, going out and waving at people and kissing babies and all that other stuff. Lehua was out there campaigning with me and my children helped get posters out.

I ran in two successive elections and in total, I must have spent $20,000 out of my own pocket. I did get some support, but not much really. Both times I was running against people who were already established, and the party was favoring the other person.

After that second loss, Lehua thought we should put a stop to it, which was a wise thing to do. Politics can be time consuming and once you start, it's hard to stop because it gets in your blood. There's a challenge and you get determined. It's similar in a way to business. You have it tough, but if you are determined and overcome those things, then you become a success.

When I first started out as a political candidate, my next-door neighbor at the time asked me if I would be interested in joining Toastmasters. I thought it was a good idea because it was a chance for me to learn the mechanics of public speaking. Sure enough, it helped me a great deal. It gave me the courage and confidence to speak in front of a group of people. I learned that the secret to public speaking is that you must be sincere. If you have ulterior motives, you will not be as effective.

Campaigning was a learning process. I had the elation of succeeding in the primary, only to lose in the general election. My second election was more successful of the two because I was better known and had more campaigning experience.

...

I had always dreamed of being a pilot and was disappointed during WWII when I lost the chance to become an Aviation Cadet. In the mid-1960s, I had the chance to take flying lessons and I decided to go ahead and do it. I completed the whole course, including the flight training and successful completion of my solo flights, but failed the written test. All I had to do to get my pilot's license was pass that written exam. I was going to go back and take it again, but my family took an extended trip around that time and by the time I got back, I lost my enthusiasm for it.

After they train you to operate the plane, the instructor grants you permission to fly solo, if he or she feels you are qualified to fly on your own. I flew solo around the Honolulu area and around Kailua. My short solo flight was from Honolulu to Kahalui, Maui.

My long solo flight was from Honolulu to Hana, at the far end of Maui. I got up early in the morning and lined up behind the big jet planes with my little Cessna 150 at the Honolulu International Airport. After sufficient clearance time had passed, I got word on my radio that it was clear for me to take off. Before you know it, I was up in the air. It was really an exhilarating experience.

Shortly after I started out, I noticed that the weather conditions looked pretty bad. As I got closer to the dark clouds, I had all kinds of thoughts in my mind. Luckily, before I got there, the thing cleared up and I ended up with clear weather all the way. The Hana airport was just a small landing field. When I was preparing to land, I noticed that there were cattle and horses grazing on the runway. Since they didn't have a control tower to radio, I had to buzz the airport, fly low to let the people know I wanted to land. They then cleared the animals so I could land safely. Once down, I had to have a paper signed by an official there to attest that I had completed my long solo flight.

The flight to Hana and back that day was quite an experience. I felt free as a bird and I got to see the beauty of the islands from a bird's eyeview. I think that making those solo flights was enough for me. I had wanted to know what it was like to be up in the sky in a plane by myself and I experienced that. It was enough; I had accomplished what I wanted to do.

...

I have been a member of the Benevolent and Protective Order of Elks for the last 32 years. From the beginning, I liked their philosophy. The Elks is both fraternal and charitable. In Hawaii, our major project is helping kids who have speech impairments. We have three full-time speech therapists that go out to help the kids. I've seen some very positive results from their efforts and it makes me feel good to be part of it.

The lodge in Kailua occupies one of the units in my business property. The rent they pay is probably less than they would pay elsewhere for a similar place, and I could get more from another tenant, but that's okay. Money is not everything; there are other considerations in life.

I have gone up the steps to the highest position within any Lodge, which carries the title of Exhalted Ruler and is held for one year. I was Exhalted Ruler from 1973-1974, 1977-1978, and 1992-1993. Some years back, I was elected to the second highest position in Hawaii, which is vice president.

The Elks is a fraternal organization and we frequently have little social get togethers. It is difficult to get members to participate, and as our members have aged, they have started to restrict their activities. I've pulled back myself in recent years. I'm not as active or as determined as I used to be.

AROUND HOME

When our first child, Mary Elizabeth Keakealani was born on April 26, 1954, it started me thinking a little more about how I was living my life.

The next year, I took my one-year-old daughter to visit my mother, who was ill at the time. She passed away one week after meeting her first grandchild. That same year, I joined AA and quit drinking. On the whole, my home life improved in almost every way after I put my drinking ways behind me.

We were fortunate to have another addition to our family on October 28, 1956, when our second daughter Thelma Leimomi was born. Our third child, Clarence Herbert, named after my father, came into the world on April 23, 1958.

In 1965, we sold our old house and used the money to build a new one. We had some extra money so we decided to take a family trip to the mainland to see the sights and visit with my father's family. Clarence was seven years old and Mary Elizabeth was twelve. We flew to San Francisco and boarded a train to Chicago. It was educational for my children and I'm glad they got to ride a train cross country.

When we arrived in Chicago, I showed my family the places I had been in my early days. Then we caught a small plane to Iowa and visited my family. After our visit, we rented a car and drove from Iowa to Los Angeles. We went through Wyoming and Yellowstone National Park, and drove down the California coast. From Los Angeles, we took a plane back to Hawaii. It was a wonderful family vacation and when we got back to Hawaii, we were able to move right into our new home.

There were many pleasant memories in that new home as our children grew up, moved out, got married, and started families of their own.

By the time I retired, Clarence had been working with me for some time and, as I hoped, he stepped in and took over my business. He wanted to run it himself so I stepped out of the picture and retired completely. That all worked out well.

In 1989, we started to build the house that Lehua and I live in now. When we built it, we thought that Clarence and his family would move into our old house, which they finally did a few years ago.

Clarence was able to get a building permit and then put up an ohana (family) building at our old house. The second house is a complete home with two baths and two bedrooms. I did all of the electrical work for the ohana myself. I wanted it to be my last big project. Everything was installed by me, outside and in. Clarence, working with an architect, designed the house and had it drawn up. It was built for us as a retirement home. It fits the spirit of ohana. It allows family to be close and it's convenient for our grandchildren to come over.

TO RUSSIA WITH LOVE

A group of us from AA, along with our spouses, took a memorable trip to Russia and the Ukraine in 1991. At the time, the two countries were part of what was then called the Soviet Union. We flew from Honolulu to Los Angeles and then non-stop to Helsinki. It was a long trip. During our flight, we were able to look down on Iceland, Norway, Sweden, and Finland. When we arrived in Helsinki, we stayed overnight before boarding the train to Moscow.

We stayed in Moscow for several days. We saw Red Square, the Kremlin, the largest bell ever cast, and Lenin's tomb, with soldiers marching and guarding it. We went through a few Russian Orthodox churches and cathedrals. I was surprised to find that none of them had chairs, benches, or anything else like that. Everybody attended services standing up.

From Moscow, we took the train to Kiev, which is in the Ukraine. From there, we took a plane to St. Petersburg, previously called Leningrad. As members of AA, we were supposed to come in and prove to others that there is some substance to the program, which was in its early stages. I had been sober for 35 years at the time.

In Moscow, we went to a meeting place in a remote part of the country and were surprised to have someone call out our names. A young Russian woman by the name Galina Chernishov, who Lehua and I had met in Seattle the previous year at the International AA Convention, greeted us.

At a meeting in Kiev, I mentioned to those attending the AA meeting that I had met up with Russians during WWII at the Elbe River in Germany. A young lady, Lilia, said that her father was in that location around that time. We got to talking and she looked at the photo I had of me posing with a Russion soldier that day in 1945. She thought it could be her father. I met up with Lilia again in Leningrad where she was a professor at the University of Leningrad. She presented me with her father's knapsack and log from WWII. It was a great honor and I now have those things put safely away with my other memorabilia.

Lehua and I invited Lilia to stay with us in Hawaii if she ever came to America. She came to stay with us in 1992 and ended up liking it so much that she tried to get employment in Hawaii. She had her credentials with her and I took her around to meet the right people at the University of Hawaii, who were interested in hiring her because of her doctorate in philosophy and Russian history.

She went through the usual application process, but it took a long time, and her visa expired during the process. She returned to Russia and continued the application process from there. Once her application was accepted, she came back to Hawaii and stayed with us for a while before eventually finding a place of her own. Lilia met a fellow professor at the University of Hawaii. He is a nice man and a member of a prominent family in Hawaii. They were married and we were invited to the wedding.

That is another good thing that happened in my life. I touched someone from a distant place like Russia. It's something that you don't dream can happen, but it does happen. As we go along in life, we influence and touch others.

NEW EXPERIENCES & OLD MEMORIES

In 1995, Lehua and I were part of a group from my old 69th Infantry Division that went on a 50th anniversary reunion tour to Europe to see the sights and retrace the steps that we took during World War II. There were about ninety of us all together, including spouses.

To start, we flew over to Great Britain. We toured around south of England and stopped to see Stonehenge. From England, we crossed the English Channel to France through the newly completed Chunnel. Once in France, we revisited Le Havre and then went on to Paris, where we enjoyed leisurely days taking in the sights and ambience of the city.

When we left France, we began to follow the route that my Division and Regiment had taken into Belgium and through the Eifel Forest. When we crossed where the Siegfried Line once stood, we got out and looked around, but we could only find traces of it. That mighty physical line of defense that once guarded the border of Germany is now virtually overgrown and obliterated by the forest that has regenerated around it.

We carried on, stopping here and there along the way. We stopped in the town of Bad Ems in Germany. Things there changed so much. It is now a beautiful, tranquil place. Much of the town was rebuilt after the war. From Bad Ems, we moved on to Leipzig and then to Berlin.

The highlight of the whole trip was meeting up again with the Russian veterans at the Elbe River on the 50th anniversary of the original meeting. It was an emotional reunion and we had a big banquet together to commemorate the event. The tour brought back a lot of memories, feelings and thoughts about the war, including the impact it had on me and so many others.

Our 1995 tour included a stop at Buchenwald, one of the famous concentration camps. We got in there and walked the grounds. By that time, all the old buildings had been demolished, but there was still evidence of where they had stood. They did have a little museum that showed what had taken place there and we went through that. They still have a crematorium left standing as a memorial. That was a sad affair. I told Lehua that I was going to go in and look through that, but she wasn't too keen on me doing that so I stayed away.

I have in my possession several WWII decorations, including the Pearl Harbor Survivor medal, which was presented to me many years after the end of the war. I also have the Great Patriotic War Medal, a Russian medal that was unofficially presented to me by a young man that I met when I was touring Russia with the AA group in 1991.

My Combat Infantry Badge means a lot to me because when I met the Russians during combat, it was quite an experience. There really weren't too many American troops that joined up with the Russians, just my outfit. The rest of the soldiers never had any contact, with the exception of some of the troops up north by Berlin.

I applied for and received the Bronze Star after the end of the war. It was awarded to anyone who had been involved with direct combat with the enemy. You didn't have to have a particular documented incident of valor as with the Congressional Medal of Honor. Just being involved with and enduring combat itself was a form of valor.

The hardship that I faced, particularly when we bivouacked in the Eifel Forest, was the hardest experience that I had to go through in my entire life. The whole three months that we were involved in combat was a great hardship, and I think my way of coping with that stress was by taking that extra drink that eventually landed me in trouble.

Our trip to Europe in 1995 brought back all of those thoughts, and more. But eventually our group left Germany and entered Switzerland, which is a breathtakingly beautiful country.

We were away on that trip for just about one month. It was one of the most memorable trips that I had in my life.

SO, THAT'S IT!

Now I volunteer at the USS *Arizona* Memorial at Pearl Harbor. I go down two or three times a week and my job is to speak to the visitors that come out. I inform them as to what took place there. I was an eyewitness to that. Many of those people thank me, as they only knew what they had read about Pearl Harbor and it may not have been much. There are a few of us survivors who volunteer at the park. It is up to survivors to perpetuate the history until we are gone.

At one Pearl Harbor Day commemoration at the USS *Arizona* Memorial, some people from the national television the 700 Club interviewed my grand-daughter and me. The next day it aired on national television show and I was able to get a taped copy of the program. Not too long after, I was speaking to a group of visitors and one person said, "Say, you were on television recently, weren't you?" People recognize me from the program and bring it up when they see me at the *Arizona* Memorial. I enjoy the time I spend assisting at the *Arizona* Memorial and I'll probably stay with that program as long as I'm physically able.

As much as I enjoy the Pearl Harbor Survivors program, my first priority will always be Alcoholics Anonymous. It is my lifelong program and it allows me to positively affect individuals as well as families. If I affect one life, one family, that's okay.

Life has come out well for me. I am so grateful for everything. My early years were more like an adventure. Life is an adventure. You go through life and at the time you might see things as difficulties. Every day you face problems, but that is all part of it. I'm very comfortable now and have the satisfaction of having accomplished many things. Sometimes we don't appreciate what all we've accomplished until we sit down and do something like this story. I see now that from humble beginnings, a person can get themselves into a better situation with determination and hard work.

A person should always bear in mind that you can accomplish anything that you set your mind to. If you want something, use common sense, don't get impatient and be persistent. It'll come as time marches on. Slowly, but surely, you will get there.

Herbert Weatherwax (left) and his brother Eddie.

In uniform, Hawaii, 1943.

Visiting Chicago, 1944.

Eifel Forest, Belgium, 1945.

Norfolk Dredge, Subic Bay, Philippines.

Official campaign photo: (clockwise from top left) Mary Elizabeth, Clarence, Thelma, Herb and Lehua.

Lehua and Herb in Russia, 1991.

Volunteering on the USS *Arizona* Memorial.

Celebrating his 95th birthday at the Pearl Harbor Visitor Center.